my guide to space exploration

# Space Su

Cherry Lake Press

Published in the United States of America by Cherry Lake Publishing Group
Ann Arbor, Michigan
www.cherrylakepublishing.com

Reading Adviser: Beth Walker Gambro, MS, Ed., Reading Consultant, Yorkville, IL
Book Design: Jennifer Wahl
Illustrator: Joseph Hatch

Photo Credits: NASA, 5; NASA, 7; Josh Valcarcel – NASA – John, 9; NASA, Public domain, via Wikimedia Commons, 11; NASA, 13; NASA/Aki Hoshide, 15; NASA, 17; NASA, 19; Public Domain, U.S. National Archives, 21; © Andrei Armiagov/Shutterstock, 23



**Cherry Lake Press** is an imprint of Cherry Lake Publishing Group

Library of Congress Cataloging-in-Publication Data has been filed and is available at catalog.loc.gov

Printed in the United States of America

table of contents



**About the author:** Samantha Bell was born and raised near Orlando, Florida. She grew up in a family of eight kids and all kinds of pets, including goats, chickens, cats, dogs, rabbits, horses, parakeets, hamsters, guinea pigs, a monkey, a raccoon, and a coatimundi. She now lives with her family in the foothills of the Blue Ridge Mountains, where she enjoys hiking, painting, and snuggling with their cats Pocket, Pebble, and Mr. Tree-Tree Triggers.

**About the illustrator:** Joseph Hatch is the art director for Tilbury House Publishers. He holds a degree in Graphic Design and Illustration from Madison College in Madison, Wisconsin. An illustrator, painter, and certified Michigan master naturalist, Joseph can usually be found at home organic gardening, beekeeping, growing edible mushrooms, planting native plants, and either building, fixing, or playing stringed instruments. He lives in Ann Arbor, Michigan, with his wife, their two children, a house cat, two dogs, nine chickens, and fifty thousand honeybees.

About Space Suits

I'm a space suit. **Astronauts** wear me.

PAYLOAD NAS
KOICHI WAKATA

We go on **space walks**.

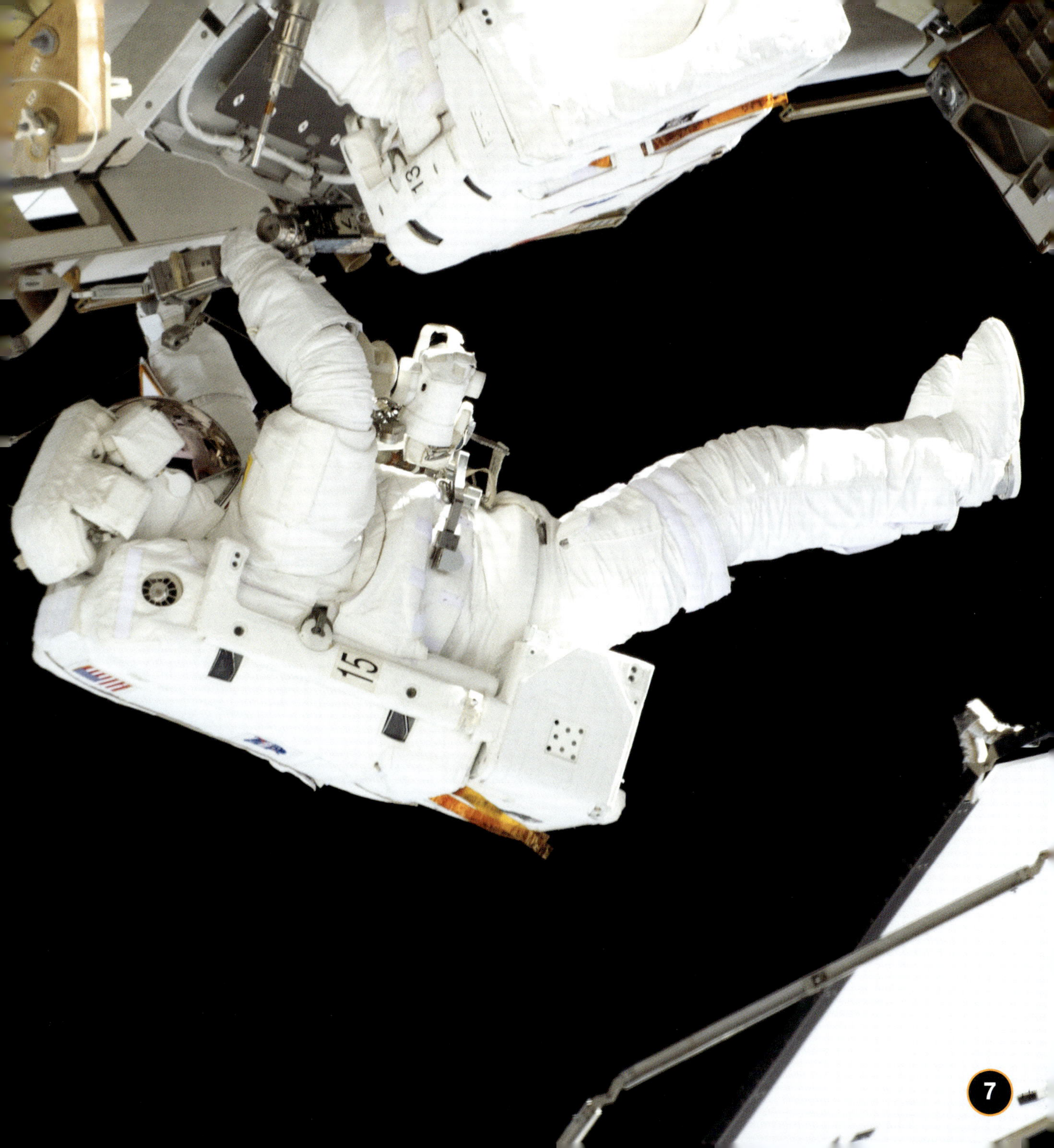
15

I have **layers**. Each layer has a job.

My first layer has tubes. The tubes have water. It keeps me cool inside.

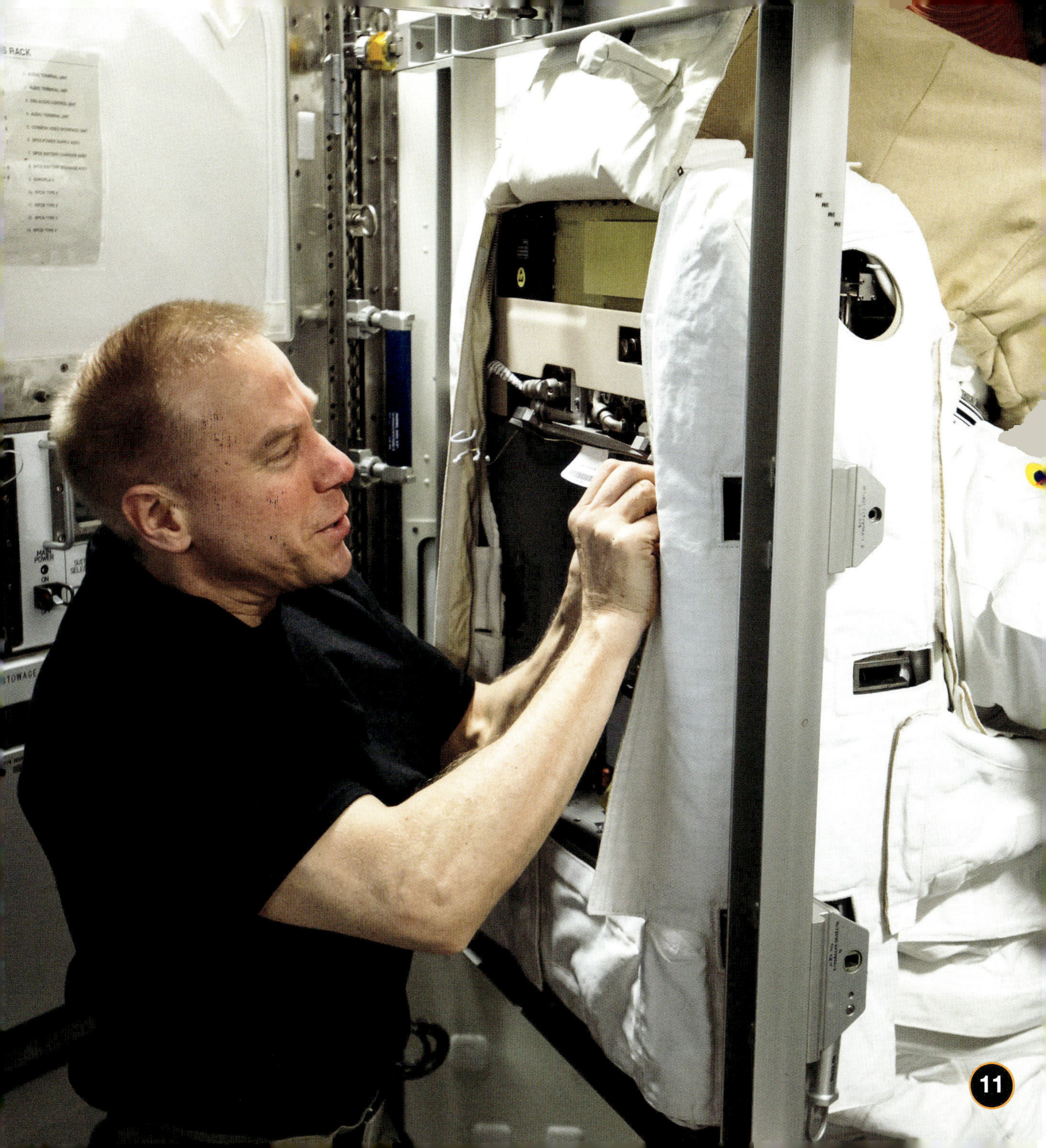

I keep astronauts safe.
I keep **pressure** steady.

My outer layer is white. It keeps the Sun's heat away. It also stops dust **particles**. Space dust moves fast. It can hurt.

3015
PORTABLE
FIRE
EXTINGUISHER
WATER
MIST PF

I have a backpack. It has **oxygen**. It has a **two-way radio**. Astronauts can talk with it.

I have a helmet. Its **visor** is gold. The visor protects eyes. The Sun is bright in space.

I also have a bag. It has water to drink.

AI
OUTBOARD
REMOVE ALL STOWED ITEMS
FROM POCKETS BEFORE LANDING
NASA
STS-115/ISS-12A

I'm like a small spacecraft!

glossary & index

## glossary

**astronauts** (AA-struh-nahts) people trained to take part in spaceflight

**layers** (LAY-urz) materials that are different from the other materials on either side

**oxygen** (AHK-suh-jin) a gas that most living things need

**particles** (PAAR-tuh-kulz) a tiny piece of something

**pressure** (PREH-shuhr) a steady force on an object

**space walks** (SPAYS WAWKS) moving around outside a spacecraft in outer space

**two-way radio** (TOO WAY RAY-dee-oh) a device that can both transmit and receive radio signals, allowing for two or more people to communicate

**visor** (VIE-zuhr) the front part of a helmet that protects the eyes and face

## index